★ ★ ★ DISCOVERIN

Remembe

By **Kristie Kiernan Bouryal**
Illustrated by **Gabe** and **Haruka Ostley**

Designed by James Johnson
www.jamesjohnson.net

Copyedited by RSH Communications

Photos on pages 30-32, 37 provided by the FDNY

Photos on pages 33-37 provided by FDNY Firefighter Daniel Alfonso
www.bigapplefirephotography.com

ISBN 978-1-7329913-1-6

This book is dedicated to first responders and all of those we loved and lost, including Fire Department of the City of New York (FDNY) members who made the supreme sacrifice in the performance of their duty at the World Trade Center on September 11, 2001 at Manhattan BOX 5-5-8087.

Chapter 1

Cousins Tyler, Olivia and Sophia smiled and looked on as dozens of people warmly said hello to each other. They were at the Rescue Company 1 firehouse memorial for September 11, 2001. People were shaking hands and many hugged and kissed Grandpa and Grandma. They could tell people were very happy to see them and it was clear these people were close to their family. They hadn't really understood the relationship their family had with the Fire Department of the City of New York (FDNY), but it quickly became obvious that this was an important part of their family's life and they were curious to know a lot more about it.

People were participating in discussions inside and outside of the firehouse. "Let's make our way inside,"

Grandpa said as Grandma reached out for Sophia's hand. As they walked toward the front window of the firehouse, a beautiful plaque captured their attention. The family came to a complete stop and gathered around it. It had pictures of 11 men with their names and the logo for Rescue 1 on the left-hand side.

"Still Riding Rescue 1, 09-11-01," Tyler read aloud. "That's what it says on the top," he told Sophia as he began to read aloud the names under each picture. "Captain Terence Hatton, Lieutenant Dennis Mojica, Firefighter Joseph Angelini, Firefighter Gary Geidel, Firefighter Patrick O'Keefe, Firefighter Michael Montesi, Firefighter Gerard Nevins, Firefighter William Henry, Firefighter David Weiss, Firefighter Kenneth Marino and Firefighter Brian Sweeney," he continued.

"That's who we are here to remember today along with many others who gave their lives on September 11, 2001. America was attacked in multiple cities that day, including here in New York City, where the famous and tall Twin Towers collapsed. The Twin Towers were part of the set of buildings known as the World Trade Center," Grandma said. "Mrs. Henry dedicated this plaque to remember the men from this firehouse who gave their lives that day. She's the mother of William, who we called Billy."

"Grandpa, were all of these men your friends?" Olivia asked softly. "Yes, they were all my friends. I also knew many others from other firehouses who made the ultimate sacrifice that day," Grandpa replied. "What's the ultimate sacrifice?" Tyler asked. Grandpa paused for a moment and then said, "Being willing to do whatever it takes, even to give their own lives, to save others," Grandpa answered.

Grandma rubbed one hand over Olivia's head and the other across Sophia's cheek. "Grandpa, can you tell us about them?" Tyler asked. "I'd like to," said Grandpa. "I'll tell you whatever you want to know."

Grandma took Sophia and Olivia's hands and walked into the firehouse. Tyler followed, ahead of Grandpa. They walked slowly through the hallway as they looked in wonder at pictures from fire and rescue scenes covering the walls. There were photos of ship, truck and car fires, water rescues and more.

"Oh wow, that fire was so huge!" exclaimed Olivia as she pointed to one of many pictures showing things burning. "Yes, I remember that fire. It was a big one," said Grandpa. "You and your friends went into these giant fires to save people, Grandpa?" asked Olivia. "Yes, Liv. We sure did," Grandpa replied. "They're so brave," said Tyler as Sophia nodded her head.

"They must be really dedicated," said Olivia. "I mean, all of these fires were so dangerous but they didn't let that stop them. They saved people and people survived because of them," she said.

Grandma led the way into the kitchen. She and Grandpa were greeted by more people as Tyler, Olivia and Sophia filled their plates with scrambled eggs and pancakes while gazing intently at more pictures on the kitchen walls.

A lot of people were visiting the firehouse that day so the Rescue 1 firetruck, also known as the rig, was in the street. Folding tables and chairs filled the firehouse where the rig would normally be parked so guests could sit, eat and visit with one another. Grandma found seats at a table and several of Grandpa and Grandma's friends sat with them and started talking to Grandpa.

Olivia was surprised. "Grandma, how do you and Grandpa know all of these people?" she asked. "Grandpa used to work with some of the firefighters here, and even ones he didn't work with, he met through the years. We met their families over the years at services like this, dinners, Christmas parties, weddings and birthdays," Grandma explained. "The fire department is like a big extended family."

"Do these people know the people we are here to remember?" Sophia asked Grandma. "Yes, Soph. In some cases, they were related to them and others were friends," Grandma said. "How were they related?" asked Tyler. "In different ways," Grandma said as she looked around the room and her eyes filled with tears. "Some of the men we lost were sons of the people here, brothers or husbands. Some worked with them, some were fathers, grandfathers, friends," Grandma replied. "No matter how the people here knew the people we lost on 9/11, you can be sure they loved them very much."

"Wow, a lot of people lost people they loved," Olivia said as she shook her head. "Yes," said Grandma, "and this is just one firehouse. This city lost a total of 343 members of the FDNY that day. A lot of people outside of the FDNY gave their lives along with many others in other cities, too. America suffered great loss on September 11, 2001."

"Grandma, that makes me feel so sad," said Sophia. "I know, Soph, it makes me feel sad, too," she said, "but that's why we have faith and why we pray for goodness to spread through the world. After September 11, 2001 goodness won and you could see that by the outpouring of kindness throughout the United States and beyond," said Grandma.

Chapter 2

Tyler looked at Grandpa across the table to get his attention. "Grandpa, what were the men like that we're here to honor?" he asked curiously. "Well, one thing I can tell you is that they were all heroes long before September 11, 2001," Grandpa said. "Together, these men served a total of 210 years in the FDNY and they were given awards for their bravery by the department 89 times. They were super firefighters."

"Now, a lot of people would call them heroes based on that alone, or because they gave their lives saving others on 9/11. But they were heroes because of the way they chose to live their lives. These were exemplary men, good, family men. Some were husbands, fathers, uncles, coaches and so much more. When they came to work, they put on their uniforms and risked their lives to save others. But at home they were helping their families, kids, friends and neighbors. They fixed fences, worked in construction, plumbing, coached games for their kids and one even had a farm. They were never looked at as everyday heroes, but that's exactly what they were. Everyday heroes are all around you in this life, but they usually don't talk about their heroic acts. You have to ask questions to uncover their stories," said Grandpa.

"What's an everyday hero?" Sophia asked. "Everyday heroes are regular people who do things that make a difference," Grandma replied. "Like a mother, father, sister or cousin who fights fires, crime, or helps people who need medical care. It could be a kid who helps a person with a disability or an elderly neighbor with their yard chores. It could even be a person who every morning smiles at people on the street just to help brighten their day. You see, an everyday hero can do something incredibly brave or simple and kind. They do what they believe is right without being told to do it and it makes a difference to others," said Grandma.

"Grandpa, can you tell me about Captain Hatton?" Olivia asked softly. "Oh, Liv," Grandpa sighed. "Terry was family to us, the best of the best. He was a dear friend, an incredible firefighter and a great leader who made all of his firefighters better," he said. "Terry was driven, loyal, disciplined and he knew the buildings of Manhattan inside and out. He was honored by the FDNY 19 times for his bravery."

"That's amazing," said Tyler. "Yeah," said Liv and Sophia with their eyes wide. "Rescue 1 covers all of Manhattan so that made him captain of this whole island. To play on his name, I nicknamed him Captain Man-Hatton, but it was very fitting. After September 11th this street was named in his honor and the rig was, too," Grandpa continued. "Terry always used the word 'outstanding' instead of words like 'good' or 'great,' so the rig is named 'Outstanding' in his memory."

"That's so cool. People must have really loved him," Olivia said in amazement. "Yes, and for good reason. He was truly an outstanding, one-of-a-kind man," said Grandpa.

"I wish I could have met him," said Tyler. "Me, too," said Sophia and Olivia. "We wish you could have as well," said Grandma. "But we can tell you more stories and also introduce you to members of his family so you can hear their perspectives." "Promise?" asked Sophia. "Absolutely. If we don't see them today, next time for sure," said Grandma.

"Grandpa did you say earlier that someone was a plumber and another person had a farm?" asked Olivia. Grandma and Grandpa laughed. "Yes, Gerry had a farm with pigs, goats and chickens. Once we visited and went pumpkin picking with his family. He used to drive a pickup truck and he was always loading it with things he could use on the farm," Grandpa said with a big smile.

"Billy loved being a fireman but he was also a contractor and a plumber on the side," Grandpa continued. "Once, our house needed some plumbing work so I asked him for advice. The next time I saw him, he brought me his special tools so I could use them for the job. It was so nice of him and his kindness saved us a lot of money. He loved vacationing, often in Brazil, and he was also a collector. He and Grandma used to talk about their latest finds."

"I can't believe he was a plumber, too? He had a lot of skills," Tyler said. "Yes, he was talented," Grandpa said. "As was Mike, who was also a plumber and who was building a house for his family when 9/11 happened. He was highly knowledgeable and a great family man and firefighter." "Wait, did he get to finish the house?" Olivia asked. "He didn't, but kind heroes came to the rescue and finished it for his family," Grandpa said. "Wow, that was so nice of them," said Olivia.

"Didn't Joe serve for something like 40 years?" Grandma asked. "Yes," Grandpa said. "He was the oldest active firefighter in the FDNY. Joe loved firefighting and being in the firehouse. He used to say great firefighters are all the same type of people; 'the faces may change but we're all the same,'" Grandpa said. "He had a son in the FDNY who was working for another firehouse. He also gave his life on 9/11," Grandma said. "That's terrible," Tyler commented as he looked at Olivia and Sophia and shook his head.

"What about the other men, Grandpa?" asked Sophia. "Well, Dennis always thought of the safety of his firefighters and taught them to act as a unit," Grandpa said. "He was a mentor to a young Danny Alfonso who was like a son to him. Danny later became a firefighter and is here today. Dennis also loved going dancing with his fiancée Maria on Saturday nights. Gary was an Eagle Scout when he was a kid and later became a Boy Scout leader. He was strong, humble, quiet, calm and always there to do whatever he could in a fire. He drove the rig for me sometimes and was scheduled to retire two weeks after September 11, 2001. He wasn't even supposed to be working that day but he decided to work overtime," said Grandpa. "Wait – he wasn't supposed to be working and then two weeks later he was supposed to retire?" Olivia asked in disbelief. "Yes," said Grandma. Liv, Tyler and Sophia shook their heads. "That's such a shame," said Tyler. "Yeah, it really is," added Sophia as Liv continued to shake her head.

"Dave saw the lighter side of things. He had fun with life, drove Harley-Davidson motorcycles and gave us some great laughs," Grandpa continued as he chuckled. "It sounds like he was funny," said Olivia. "He was but when that alarm went off and we headed to a fire, he was all business," Grandpa said. "So was Kenny. He was a true professional and another great talent in the firehouse. Just say the word and he was on it. He was a loving family man like the rest of these guys, too," said Grandpa.

"Grandpa, they all sound so nice. Like people I would really like to know," said Tyler. "You would have loved them," Grandpa replied. "Tell us about the others," said Sophia.

"Brian was young, energetic and looking to be successful in the FDNY, following in the footsteps of his father, Ed. He loved outdoor activities, especially snowboarding," Grandpa said. "Now, Paddy wasn't an outspoken person but when he spoke, he commanded attention. He was experienced, talented and could handle any situation. He worked a lot in construction on the side and enjoyed sailing,"

Grandpa told them. "Sailing?" asked Sophia. "Yeah, boats," Tyler said with a big smile. "That must have been so cool."

"That's a little about the men from Rescue 1 who gave their lives that day," Grandpa said. "But many others did, too, including firefighters from other houses. Like one of my closest friends, Mike Esposito from Squad 1," Grandpa said.

"One of your closest friends? What was he like?" asked Tyler. "He was simply the best," Grandpa said. "An exceptional firefighter who always found a way to get the job done. He could make anyone laugh and I don't mean giggle. I mean doubled over with pain in your stomach, crying laughing. He never laughed at people, he laughed with them and lifted their spirits. You should ask your mothers about some of his stories," he said as he laughed heartily. "We spent a lot of time together. We worked together, car-pooled, worked out, studied, got promoted and we played jokes on people together," he said laughing. "When we worked at Rescue 2 on Bergen Street, the guys used to call us the 'Bergen Street Bookends,' or even more famously, 'Two Bodies, One Brain,'" Grandpa said as the whole family burst out laughing.

Chapter 3

People started to leave their seats to gather in front of the firehouse for the memorial ceremony. Grandma and Grandpa quickly cleaned up the breakfast dishes and showed Tyler, Olivia and Sophia outside where they stood in front of the large group of people. They were facing the rig and people lined up near it, including Grandpa.

"Grandma, why aren't they standing with us?" asked Sophia. "They are part of the ceremony," Grandma said as the group became silent and focused their attention on the current captain of Rescue 1. He welcomed and thanked everyone there, those in front of the firehouse and even people passing on the street who stopped to pay their respects.

The group then joined in an opening prayer, followed

by naming, one-by-one, the 11 fallen members of Rescue Company 1.

Captain Terence Hatton.
Lieutenant Dennis Mojica.
Firefighter Joseph Angelini.
Firefighter Gary Geidel.
Firefighter Patrick O'Keefe.
Firefighter Michael Montesi.
Firefighter Gerard Nevins.
Firefighter William Henry.
Firefighter David Weiss.
Firefighter Kenneth Marino.
Firefighter Brian Sweeney.

Next, the group joined in a moment of silence in their honor. Tyler, Olivia and Sophia bowed their heads in silence along with Grandma, Grandpa and all of the other attendees.

Monsignor Frank C. McGrath, who was the priest for Rescue 1 on September 11, 2001 and who spoke at most of the fallen's funerals and memorials, then spoke about the lives of the brave and courageous men. Tyler, Olivia and Sophia saw many people wiping away tears, including Grandma, while others looked sad and expressionless, like Grandpa.

The ceremony concluded with a bagpiper playing a traditional, touching song, as everyone stood at attention, remembering the heroes.

Grandpa walked from the rig to Grandma and gave her a kiss on the cheek and a hug, as she fought back tears. "That was very moving," said Tyler. "It really was," added Liv.

"I feel sad," said Sophia, "but I am so glad we are here." "We're glad you are here experiencing this, too," Grandma said. "OK. Now it's time for a group family hug," she said as they all smiled and hugged one another. Soon, members of their fire department family joined in the hug. Frowns became smiles as they embraced and helped to lift each other's spirits.

Chapter 4

The family talked and caught up with friends for the next hour. Then it was time to leave and pay their respects at another firehouse where Grandpa worked, Rescue Company 2 in Brooklyn, New York. Grandpa was driving with Grandma in the front seat and Tyler, Olivia and Sophia in the back.

"So, what do you think about today so far? Was it what you expected?" Grandma asked. "It was so much more than I imagined it would be. I can't believe how much I learned," Tyler said. "Yeah, and I can't believe how brave and heroic those men were," said Liv. "I mean, I feel like they were so special that there should be books and movies about them because there's so much more I want to know." Grandma and Grandpa glanced at each other and smiled.

"John, slow down! Look!" Grandma exclaimed. "Kids, look at the people cheering with the signs on the side of the road," she said.

Tyler started reading the signs aloud, "Thank you. God Bless America. Keep it Up." Olivia shouted, "Look at all the flags! Oh, and look at that sign: We Will Never Forget You!"

"Oh, wow. They're re-enacting what they did for first responders after September 11th," Grandpa said as his voice shook. "They're showing all the cars on the road what they did back then." He began honking his horn and rolled down the windows. "Thank you! Thank you!" he yelled. "Thank you!" Grandma yelled as she waved her arms. The kids yelled, too, "Thank you! Thank you!"

As the cheering faded, Grandpa put the windows up. "Grandpa, I don't understand. What are they re-enacting?" Tyler asked.

"The road we are on was closed to regular traffic and only used to move first responders to and from Ground Zero. Ground Zero is what we called the World Trade Center site after the Twin Towers fell," Grandpa replied. "Now imagine that as a first responder you are helping to move giant pieces of debris and giant steel beams, even digging through the rubble with your hands. You're searching for hours and hours while inhaling smoke and World Trade Center dust, which is what formed when the contents of the buildings were crushed. The site was vast and the work was painstaking, but not just because it took a lot out of us physically. It took an emotional toll on us because most of us lost many people we loved. We

were devastated."

"I remember feeling very alone, even though there were a lot of people there with me at Ground Zero. But after a long day of that, I remember getting on a city bus that was only being used for first responders. As the bus started driving on the road, I saw rows and rows of people lining

the sides of the streets. They were cheering and waving signs like the ones you just saw. They were doing that to help lift our spirits because they knew we were dealing with the darkest hours and days of our lives. They called this part of the road Hero Highway. It gave me chills every time I experienced it, and it still does today. They were thanking us and all I wanted to do was thank them. It meant so much to me and so many others. Words don't seem enough to describe what that felt like and what that meant to us," said Grandpa.

"Oh wow, how did they even think to do that?" asked Tyler. "I don't know," Grandma told him, "but isn't it great that they thought of it, did it for many months and re-enact it all these years later? It's awesome," she said. "It's so crazy because they were thanking you for being heroes, but really they were heroes for you, right, Grandpa?" Olivia asked. "That's exactly right, Liv. It's what we were talking about before. Their actions had a huge, positive impact on so many, including me. They were everyday heroes helping us. I wish I knew their names and could personally thank every one of them," he said.

"Oh man, there's just so much to learn and so much more I want to know," Tyler said. "I want to learn more, too," said Liv. "Me, too," said Sophia.

"You're right about that. There's a lot more for you to learn. But we can tell you more and Grandpa and I know the perfect places we can take you to," said Grandma. "Yep. We know the perfect places," Grandpa said as he smiled at Grandma.

"You do?" asked Tyler. "Are they near here? Can we go now?" Olivia asked.

"They are near here, but we should go on another day when we have more time," Grandpa said. "They are very special places that were created to remember and honor the people who gave their lives on September 11, 2001," he said.

"I can't wait. I hope we can go soon," Tyler said. "Me, too," said Sophia and Olivia. "Thank you for bringing us today and helping us to understand this, Grandma and Grandpa," said Olivia. "Yeah, thank you," added Sophia. "Thanks, love you," Tyler chimed in.

"You're welcome. We love you, too, and are looking forward to you learning a lot more. You know, we're going to need your help explaining all of this to your baby cousin Thomas," said Grandma. "Oh no! He is only a few months old and he doesn't know any of this!" Sophia exclaimed as she giggled. "Oh, man, this is just crazy," Tyler said as he placed his hands on the top of his head.

"You're going to be able to help him understand like we're helping you," Grandpa said. "Yes, and we will," Liv said excitedly. "When he is a little older we can go to the Rescue 1 memorial with him, then we can tell him about Hero Highway and we can take him to the special places we are going to next," she said. "Yeah, and we can tell him about all the people we met, too," added Sophia. "Yes, you can do all of that and more for him," said Grandma.

"I am so proud of you for being so excited to learn more about September 11, 2001. It was an important day in our country's history and a day that changed many lives forever. It's important that you understand what we experienced so you can help others understand and never forget," Grandpa said. "Oh, we will," said Sophia. "We have to," said Liv. "Definitely we will Grandpa, don't worry about that. We'll never forget," Tyler said as Grandma and Grandpa looked at each other and smiled.

Join Tyler, Olivia and Sophia as they learn more about September 11, 2001. In the next book in the *Discovering Heroes*™ series, Grandpa and Grandma take them to very special places that were created to remember and honor the people who gave their lives on September 11, 2001. Visit www.contextproductions.com.

Word List

'Remembering Heroes'

This book contains some phrases and words that you may not be familiar with, so Grandma and Grandpa explain what they mean in this word list, also known as a glossary of terms, you can refer to as a reminder.

Manhattan BOX 5-5-8087

This is an example of the special language or codes the FDNY uses for emergencies. The numbers indicate the seriousness of the situation and its location so the FDNY can get the right people there. On September 11, 2001, this is the code that was given to the situation at the World Trade Center.

Logo

A logo is a symbol or a design that helps you remember something. In this story, the logo in the plaque represents Rescue Company 1.

Dedicated

The word dedicated is used in two different ways in this book. In one part, Grandma explains that Mrs. Henry dedicated the plaque in the front window of the firehouse, which means she gave or donated it to honor the fallen men. In another part of the book, Olivia comments about how dedicated the firefighters must be. Here, she means the firefighters are devoted, or committed to a task or purpose, like saving people and putting out fires.

Exemplary

When Grandpa describes the fallen as exemplary men, he means the men were the best, role models, people others should admire and praise.

Perspectives

Perspectives are points of view or thoughts people may have about someone or something.

First Responder

A first responder is a man or woman who takes action in emergency situations to try to help and/or rescue people in danger. Firefighters, police and emergency personnel are all examples of first responders.

Painstaking

By painstaking, Grandpa meant the work at Ground Zero was extremely difficult, dangerous and required very close attention.

Debris

Debris is pieces of the buildings and other broken materials spread out across the large area where the buildings once stood.

Rubble

Pieces of the buildings that collapsed and everything that was in them may also be called rubble.

Vast

When Grandpa said the site was vast, he meant it was huge, like if you stood at one end you wouldn't even be able to see the other side.

Devastated

Devastated means feeling shocked or deeply saddened, which is how Grandpa and countless others felt at Ground Zero on September 11, 2001 and afterwards; even people who weren't at Ground Zero felt devastated by what happened.

Meet the Heroes

Special thanks to the FDNY for allowing us to print photos of the men named in this book. These heroes made the supreme sacrifice in the performance of their duty at the World Trade Center on September 11, 2001 at Manhattan BOX 5-5-8087. We will never forget.

Captain
Terence Hatton
FDNY Rescue 1

Lieutenant
Dennis Mojica
FDNY Rescue 1

Firefighter
Joseph Angelini
FDNY Rescue 1

**Firefighter
Gary Geidel
FDNY Rescue 1**

**Firefighter
Patrick O'Keefe
FDNY Rescue 1**

**Firefighter
Michael Montesi
FDNY Rescue 1**

**Firefighter
Gerard Nevins
FDNY Rescue 1**

**Firefighter
William Henry
FDNY Rescue 1**

**Firefighter
David Weiss
FDNY Rescue 1**

**Firefighter
Kenneth Marino
FDNY Rescue 1**

**Firefighter
Brian Sweeney
FDNY Rescue 1**

**Lieutenant
Michael Esposito***
FDNY Squad 1

**Joseph Angelini, Jr.
FDNY Ladder
Company 4**

* Lieutenant Michael Esposito was promoted to captain after his death.

Inside FDNY's Rescue Company 1

Big thanks to FDNY Firefighter Daniel Alfonso. He took these pictures to show you inside the real Rescue Company 1. You can see more of his amazing fire photos at www.bigapplefirephotography.com.

Hanging in the front window of the firehouse, a plaque honors the members of Rescue 1 who gave their lives on September 11, 2001.

Pictures showing the skill and years of experience that Rescue 1 is known for line the walls of the front entrance.

The photos show Rescue 1 members fighting fires, responding to emergencies and greeting U.S. Presidents. The opposite wall displays praise from the FDNY for Rescue 1's exceptional work.

At the top left is the original Rescue 1 firehouse on 43rd Street in New York City before it was destroyed by fire and rebuilt.

In the kitchen, members of Rescue 1 are surrounded

by pictures of current and past members at fires, emergencies and official functions, like FDNY Medal Day and parades. Above the photos is a wooden Rescue 1 logo which honors the creation of Rescue 1 on March 8, 1915. Rescue 1 has served New York City for over 100 years.

On the back wall of the kitchen is the front of what used to be the original Rescue 1 firehouse. It was saved when the firehouse was destroyed by fire. The large wooden table has the names of Rescue 1 members who gave their lives on September 11, 2001 written in gold letters. The table was donated to Rescue 1 and it serves as a reminder to all who see it.

Outside of Rescue 1, 43rd Street is named in honor of Captain Terence Hatton.

Credit: FDNY

After September 11, 2001, the Rescue 1 rig was named "Outstanding" in honor of Captain Terence Hatton.

About Grandpa

Grandpa is a loving husband, a father to four daughters and a grandfather to four grandchildren. He is a former lieutenant in the Fire Department of the City of New York, where he valiantly served for nearly 25 years. For about 17 of those years, he was assigned to three of the department's five elite rescue units - Rescue 1, Rescue 2 and Rescue 5.

About Grandma

Grandma is a loving wife, a kind, giving and thoughtful mother to four daughters and a grandmother to four grandchildren. She is also a former nurse who helped care for countless people throughout her life.

About Tyler, Olivia and Sophia

Tyler is an 11-year-old sixth grader with an infectious spirit and smile who loves America, his family, baseball, football, Fortnite, fishing and being creative.

Olivia is a bright-eyed, determined, 9-year-old third grader who loves an intellectual challenge, art, baking, sports, dance and video on demand.

Sophia is a witty, playful 6-year-old first grader with a sheepish smile and a sly spirit who loves animals, music, cooking, swimming, gymnastics, mobile devices and video on demand.

About the Author

Kristie Kiernan Bouryal is an author and an accomplished communication and marketing strategist with more than 25 years of experience building brands, demand and revenue generation across multiple industries. She has a proven track record of success in executive roles spanning global corporate communications, marketing and all forms of media.

Kristie has received numerous awards and recognition throughout her distinguished career, including an International Business Award for Brand Renovation from the Stevie® Awards; Gold Quill Excellence Awards from The International Association of Business Communicators; multiple Gold Hermes Creative Awards from the Association of Marketing and Communication Professionals; the Chairman's Prize for Innovation at The Associated Press; and the news industry's prestigious Peabody Award.

Kristie is a graduate of Syracuse University's S.I. Newhouse School of Public Communications. She is a loving wife, sister, aunt and the oldest of four girls born to a now retired nurse and a former lieutenant in the Fire Department of the City of New York's elite rescue units. Kristie was born and raised in Staten Island, New York and currently resides in New Jersey with her husband.

About the Illustrators

Gabe Ostley was born in Minnesota and graduated from the Savannah College of Art and Design with a B.F.A. degree in Sequential Art. After working in illustration and licensed characters in New York, New York, he moved to Hong Kong where he was artist-in-residence for the Yew Chung Education Foundation. There, his work expanded to include painting, art installation, murals and large-scale sculptures. While still in Hong Kong, his comic book work was published by DC Comics, Devil's Due, and numerous indie publishers and anthologies. Recently, he adapted Declan Greene's play "Moth" into a graphic novel for The Cincinnati Review. In 2018, with his artist wife Haruka, the two formed Gabruka House in Portland, Oregon. Their all ages fantasy graphic novel project, Bokura, is a Portland Regional Arts & Culture Council grant winner.

Haruka Ashida Ostley is a multidisciplinary artist (painter/muralist/mosaic artist/performer) who was born in Japan but grew up living on four different continents with her family. After graduating from Savannah College of Art and Design with a B.F.A. in Painting, she moved to New York City, where she trained at the Stella Adler Studio of

Acting. Later, she became an artist-in-residence in Hong Kong before moving back to the USA in 2015. Currently, she works in Portland, Oregon as a freelance artist creating murals, paintings, graphic novels and commissioned portraits

Haruka enjoys working with people of different backgrounds across different media around the world. When stories and energies fill her heart, she responds with her brush, color, body, and soul.

www.gabeostley.crevado.com | www.ru-ostley.com
www.gabrukahouse.com

CPSIA information can be obtained
at www.ICGtesting.com
Printed in the USA
LVHW072039110319
610189LV00020B/733/P

* 9 7 8 1 7 3 2 9 9 1 3 1 6 *